Mapping My Country

Written by **Jen Green**

Illustrated by **Sarah Horne**

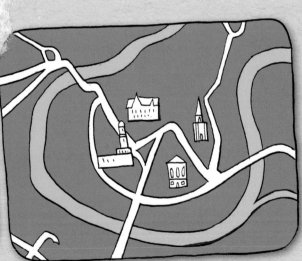

Published in paperback in 2017 by Wayland
Copyright © Hodder and Stoughton 2017

Wayland
Carmelite House
50 Victoria Embankment
London EC4Y 0DZ

MIX
Paper from
responsible sources
FSC® C104740
FSC
www.fsc.org

Series editor: Victoria Brooker
Editor: Carron Brown
Designer: Krina Patel

A CIP catalogue record for this book is available
from the British Library. Dewey number: 526-dc23
ISBN 978 0 7502 919 34
Ebook: 978 0 7502 9120 0

Printed in China

1 3 5 7 9 10 8 6 4 2

Picture acknowledgements
Front cover: top right British Library/Robana/REX; bottom centre Ashley Cooper/
SpecialistStoc/REX. Back cover: top left Shutterstock.com; bottom right Shutterstock.com.
Pages: 4 NASA; 9 Skyscan.co.uk/© R West; 10 Shutterstock.com; 11 Shutterstock.com;
14 Shutterstock.com; 25 Shutterstock.com; 28 British Library/Robana/REX;
29 left: British Library/Robana/REX; 29 right: Alex Sergre/REX.

The website addresses (URLs) included in this book were valid
at the time of going to press. However, it is possible that contents
or addresses may change following the publication of this book.
No responsibility for any such changes can be accepted by
either the author or the Publisher.

Wayland, part of Hachette Children's Group
and published by Hodder and Stoughton Limited
www.hachette.co.uk

Contents

MY COUNTRY ON THE MAP

Britain is my country. The British Isles are made up of two large islands: Great Britain and Ireland. Great Britain contains England, Wales and Scotland. Ireland contains the Republic of Ireland and Northern Ireland, which is part of the UK.

This photo of the British Isles was taken by a satellite. The white patches are clouds.

The British Isles are surrounded by water. The North Sea and English Channel separate Britain from the rest of Europe. The Irish Sea lies between Great Britain and Ireland.

What are maps?

The map below shows the British Isles. Maps show the landscape from above, like the view from a plane.

Map of the British Isles.

North Sea

Republic of Ireland

Irish Sea

Great Britain

English Channel

Maps contain all sorts of information about places, and what goes on there.

Most maps have a title, which explains what the map shows.

TRY THIS!

Compare the photo and the map of the British Isles. Which is clearer? Which is more useful? Maps don't show temporary features such as clouds. Map labels provide extra information.

COUNTRIES, CITIES AND CAPITALS

The proper name for Britain is the United Kingdom – UK for short. The UK is made up of four countries: England, Scotland, Wales and Northern Ireland. Each country has its own capital city, the home of government.

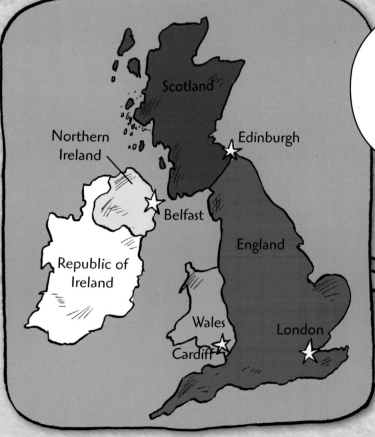

The Republic of Ireland is not part of the UK – it is a separate country, with its own capital, Dublin.

This map shows the countries of the UK and their capitals.

Cities and population

The UK has more than 64 million people. England has the largest population, with 56 million people. Britain has many large cities, such as Birmingham, Leeds, Glasgow and Sheffield. London is the biggest city of all, with over 8 million people.

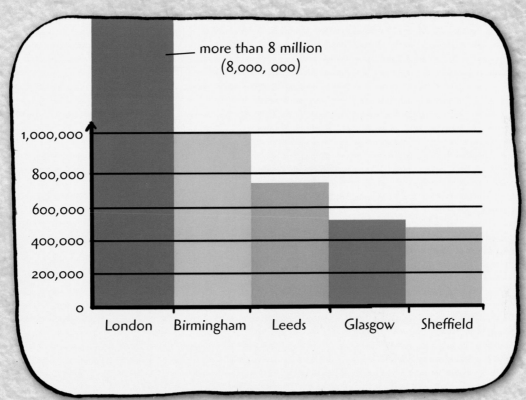

This chart shows the populations of UK's five largest cities.

TRY THIS!

Look at the map opposite and and fill in the blanks:

- ... is the capital of Northern Ireland.
- Cardiff is the capital of ...
- ... is the UK's largest city.

PHYSICAL MAPS

Maps show many different kinds of information. Political maps like the one on page 6 show countries and their borders. Physical maps like the one below show features such as rivers, lakes, seas and mountains.

Loch Ness

River Spey

Loch Lomond

River Bann

River Tay

Lough Neagh

River Tyne

River Tees

River Trent

River Great Ouse

Lake Bala

River Wye

River Severn

River Thames

Rivers are usually shown as blue lines on maps. Lakes and seas are also coloured blue.

This map shows the UK's longest rivers and largest lakes.

Rivers and lakes

Rivers and lakes contain fresh water. Britain has many rivers, such as the Thames, Humber, Tees and Tyne. Britain's longest river is the Severn, which flows through Wales and England. The UK's largest lake is Lough Neagh in Northern Ireland. Scottish lakes include Loch Lomond and Loch Ness. Lake Bala is the largest lake in Wales.

This chart shows the UK's five longest rivers.
Figures show the rivers' length in kilometres.

Loch Lomond, one of Scotland's lakes

TRY THIS!

Look at a map of your area. Which are the biggest rivers? Make your own map of the region's rivers by tracing or copying a local map. You could also show any lakes or the sea. Mark towns on rivers or the coast.

PLACES TO VISIT

Britain has thousands of amazing places to visit. As well as natural wonders such as lakes and mountains, there are also castles and historic cities such as Oxford, Bath and Edinburgh. Every year, these places attract millions of tourists, both from Britain and abroad.

Stonehenge is a historic sight in England.

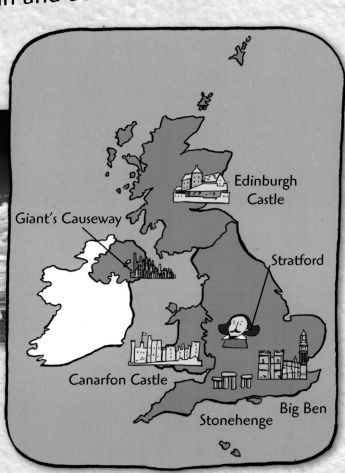

Giant's Causeway

Edinburgh Castle

Stratford

Canarfon Castle

Stonehenge

Big Ben

This map shows some of Great Britain's tourist sights.

The sights of London include Big Ben, St Paul's and Tower Bridge. Scotland, Wales and Northern Ireland have beautiful lakes, mountains and castles.

Tourist maps

Visitors use tourist maps to explore new places. These maps show famous buildings and sights in little pictures. The pictures make it easy to spot places on the map and also recognise them in real life, when you arrive.

The Giant's Causeway is an amazing stretch of coast in Northern Ireland.

TRY THIS!

Find out about places to visit in your area. Make a tourist-style map showing the attractions in pictures. Or you might be able to print small pictures or photos from the Internet to stick on your map.

READING MAPS

Tourist maps show places in little pictures, but that can make the map look crowded. Most maps use special signs called symbols instead of pictures.

> Map symbols provide a lot of information about people and places, but keep the map simple, so it is easy to read.

A tourist map of Shrewsbury.

Map symbols

There are several different types of map symbols. Coloured lines show rivers, roads and railways. Coloured areas show places such as lakes and woodlands.

Some landmarks are shown as letters, such as P for Parking. There are also very simple pictures – for example, a fish symbol means a place where you can fish.

The key at the side shows the meaning of the symbols. Not all maps use the same symbols, so it's important to check the key.

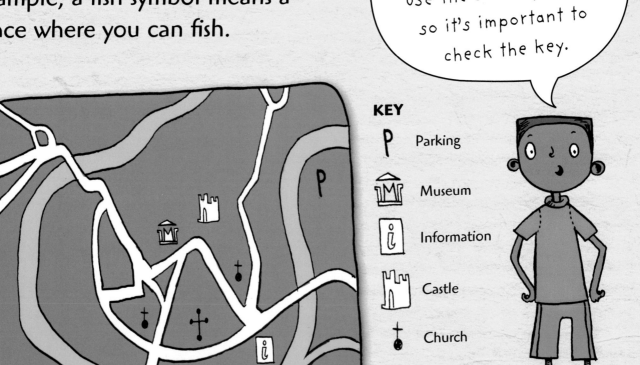

A tourist map of Shrewsbury with symbols and a key.

KEY

P   Parking

Museum

Information

Castle

Church

Cathedral

TRY THIS!

Compare the two maps here. Which is clearest? Which map has the most information? Now find a map at home and study the symbols. Do you understand all the symbols? If not, check the key.

COASTS AND ISLANDS

The UK has over 17,000 km (11,000 miles) of coastline. The British coastline is very varied, with towering cliffs, muddy river mouths, sandy beaches, bays and rocky headlands. All these features are shown on maps.

Bedruthan Steps, Cornwall

KEY

Beach

Cliff

Mud

Lighthouse

This map shows the coast of Cornwall.

Nowhere in the UK is more than 113 km (70 miles) from the sea. A third of all the people in Britain live on or near the coast, where we use the sea for food, transport and to enjoy on holiday.

Islands

The British Isles include hundreds of smaller islands as well as the two main islands. Scotland has over 700 islands. Nearly a hundred have people living on them. Scotland has three large groups of islands: the Hebrides, Orkney and Shetland.

KEY

- Channel Islands
- Hebrides
- Orkney
- Shetland
- Anglesey
- Isle of Wight
- Isle of Man

Ireland

Great Britain

Anglesey and the Isle of Man lie between Great Britain and Ireland.

TRY THIS!

Do you live on the coast? Find out about the nearest coastline at the library or using the Internet. What is the scenery like – are there cliffs or beaches? Are there towns and cities? How do people use the coast?

MOUNTAINS AND CONTOURS

Britain has many mountain ranges, particularly in Wales and Scotland. Ben Nevis in Scotland is Britain's highest peak, 1,344 metres above sea level. Snowdon is the highest peak in Wales, while Sca Fell Pike is the highest point in England.

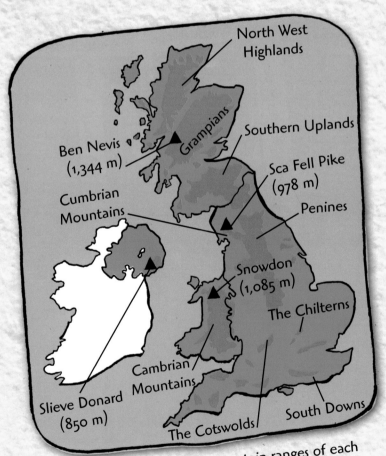

North West Highlands

Ben Nevis (1,344 m)

Grampians

Southern Uplands

Sca Fell Pike (978 m)

Penines

Cumbrian Mountains

Snowdon (1,085 m)

The Chilterns

Cambrian Mountains

Slieve Donard (850 m)

The Cotswolds

South Downs

The highest peaks and mountain ranges of each of the countries of Great Britain.

Most of eastern and southern Britain is fairly flat, with rolling hills.

18

Showing height on maps

Peaks, mountain ranges and valleys are hard to show on the flat surface of a map. Some maps show the height of the land in colour. Mountains are often coloured brown or purple, and lowlands are often green. Other maps use lines called contours, which join places at the same height above sea level.

KEY
- Above 800 m
- 500–800 m
- Below 500 m
- ▲ Mountain

If contour lines are close together, the land slopes steeply. If they are widely spaced, the land is fairly flat.

KEY
Contour line

Braeriach (1,295 m)

Cairn Gorm (1,245 m)

Ben Avon (1,171 m)

Ben MacDui (1,309 m)

Sgor an Lochain Uaine (1,258 m)

Cairn Toul (1,291 m)

The peaks of the Cairngorm mountains.

Ben Nevis

Contour map showing Ben Nevis

TRY THIS!

Look at the map opposite and answer these questions:

- What is the name of the main mountain range in Wales?
- Name the mountain range that contains Ben Nevis.
- Name a line of hills in southern Britain.

NORTH, SOUTH, EAST AND WEST

We use the points of the compass to tell which way we are facing. The four main compass points are north, south, east and west. Compass directions are shown on most maps.

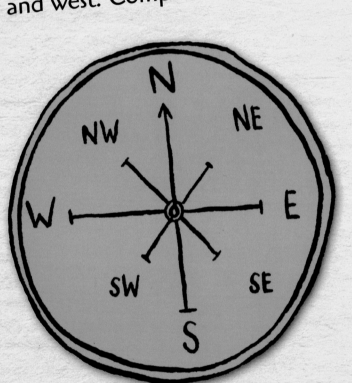

You can use a map and a real compass to find your way on a walk. The magnetic needle on the compass always points to north.

Furthest north and south

The most northerly point on the UK mainland is Dunnet Head near John O' Groats in Scotland. The most southerly point in mainland Britain is Lizard Point in Cornwall. It's over 1,300 km (800 miles) from John O' Groats to Lizard Point. That would take you 30-40 days to walk!

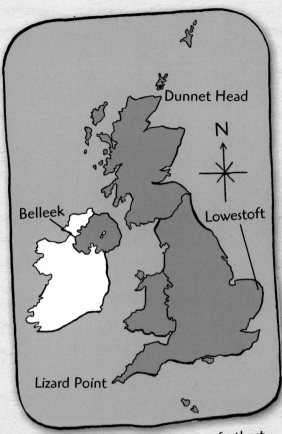

This map shows the points furthest north, south, east and west in Britain.

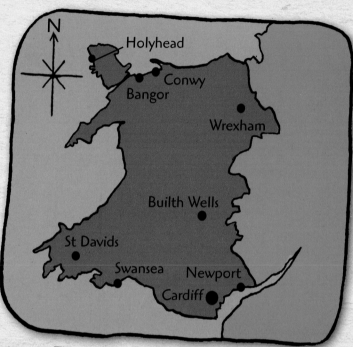

This is a map of Wales with key towns.

TRY THIS!

You can use compass directions to explain where places are in relation to one another. For example on the map of Wales, Cardiff is southeast of Swansea. Look at the map and fill in the blanks:

- Holyhead is ... of Conwy.
- Swansea lies ... of Bangor.
- The city of ... lies south of Builth Wells.

UK IN A GRID

Many UK and also local maps have lines running up, down and across the page. The lines make squares that form a grid. On the map below the squares running across the page have letters, and ones running up have numbers.

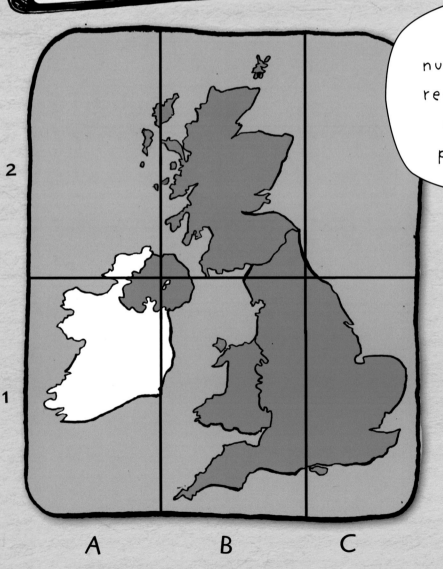

The letters and numbers make a grid reference, which you can use to locate places on the map.

Reading the grid

Grid references are always read in a certain order. Put your finger at the bottom left hand corner of the map, and run it across the page to read a letter. Then run it up the page to read the number. This gives a reference such as B1 on the map below.

You can remember the order by saying: 'ALONG the corridor and then UP the stairs'.

TRY THIS!

Look at the grid map of Northern Ireland. Can you answer these questions?

• Northern Ireland's highest mountain is in square C1. What is its height?
• What is the name of the UK's biggest lake, in squares B1 and B2?
• Give the grid reference for city of Belfast.

WEATHER MAPS

The weather in the UK is always changing. Quite often we get sunshine, clouds and rain all in one day. We also get thunderstorms, and frost, snow and hail in winter.

Weather forecasts tell us what the weather will be like, which helps us to plan our day. These forecasts are shown on maps.

KEY

Sun

Rain

Cloud

Sun with cloud

Weather symbols

Weather maps use special symbols to show sunshine, clouds, rain and other weather conditions. The key explains the symbols. Some weather maps give other kinds of information, for example, summer or winter temperatures, or the total rainfall in a year.

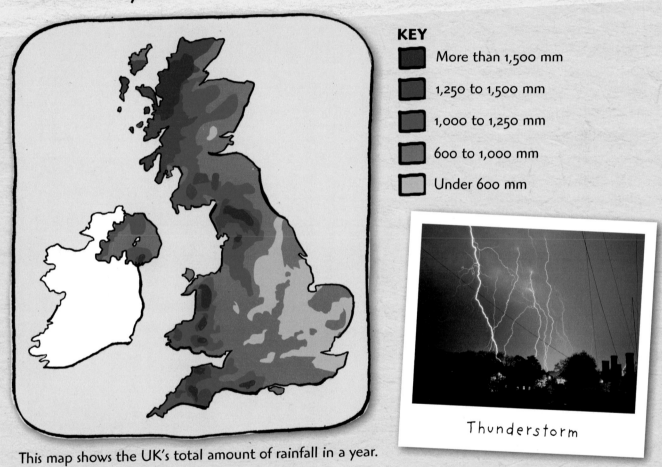

KEY

More than 1,500 mm

1,250 to 1,500 mm

1,000 to 1,250 mm

600 to 1,000 mm

Under 600 mm

Thunderstorm

This map shows the UK's total amount of rainfall in a year.

TRY THIS!

Look at or listen to the weather forecast every day for a week. Keep your own weather diary using weather symbols. Was the forecast always right?

UK, EUROPE AND THE WORLD

The UK is part of Europe. Europe has a complicated shape, as you can see on the map below. There are many islands, and large peninsulas jutting out into the sea. There are high mountain ranges such as the Alps, and long rivers such as the Danube.

KEY

River ~~~

Lake

Mountains over 5,000 m

Land from 200– 5,000 m high

Land from 0–200 m high

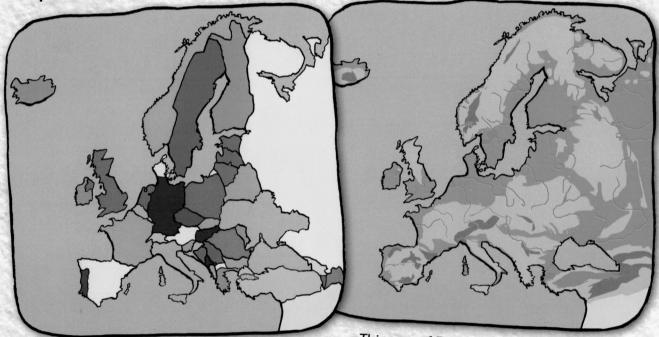

This political map shows the countries of Europe. Europe has about 50 countries including the UK.

This map of Europe shows physical features such as rivers, lakes and mountains.

Europe is one of the world's seven continents. Earth's continents are mostly separated by sea, but Europe and Asia are joined by land but separated by a line of mountains.

Maps of the world

Planet Earth is round, like a football. Only a round globe can show the true shape of the world.

> It is hard to show the true shapes of continents on the flat surface of a map.

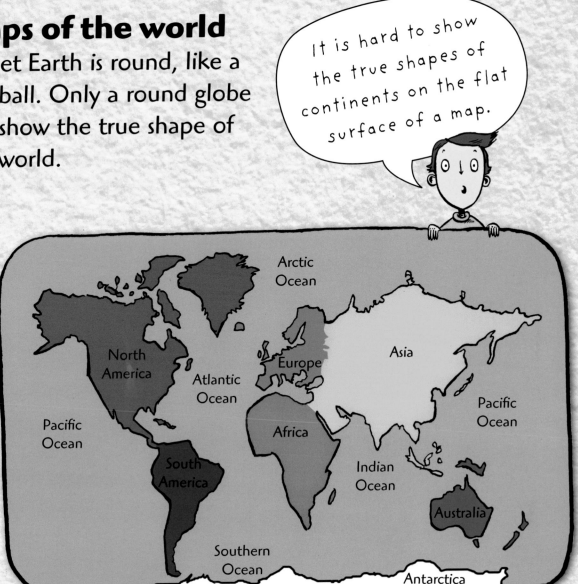

This world map shows the seven continents and five oceans.

TRY THIS!

Log on to GoogleEarth using a computer at home, school or at your local library. Use the zoom tool to zoom up on the UK, Europe and other locations. The world is a huge place, but you can explore any part of it using a computer.

MAPS OLD AND NEW

People have made maps for centuries. In days gone by, map makers would climb to the top of a hill or tower and draw the view. Later, planes were used to get a better view of the landscape. Old maps weren't very accurate.

A map of the city of London in 1572.

Modern maps are made using pictures from planes and satellites. The information is fed into a powerful computer, which produces the map.

New technology

New technology provides us with modern, interactive maps. Motorists use a tool called satellite navigation – sat nav for short. Information from satellites is used to make a map that changes as you travel, and shows your exact position. The system tells you which way to go.

In the 1500s, maps of the world changed as new lands were discovered.

Map on a mobile phone

TRY THIS!

Many mobile phones have an application with maps of cities and the countryside. The map shows your position, which helps you find your way on a walk. Try going for a walk using a map on a mobile phone.

What the words mean

Accurate Of something that is correct or right.

Capital A city that is the home of the country's government.

Compass A tool that shows directions and helps you find your way.

Continent A huge landmass. Earth has seven continents: North America, South America, Europe, Asia, Africa, Australia and Antarctica.

Contour lines Lines on a map that show the height above sea level.

Grid Squares on a map made by lines running up, down and across the page.

Grid reference Directions provided by the grid on a map.

Locate To find.

Key A panel on a map that shows the meaning of symbols.

Peninsula An area of land mostly surrounded by water.

Physical map A map that shows countries and their borders.

Political map A map that shows physical features such as rivers, lakes and mountains.

Scale The size a map is drawn to.

Symbol A sign or picture that stands for something in real life.

More information

Books

Marta Segal Block and
Daniel R Block,
Reading Maps
(Heinemann, 2008)

Cath Senker,
My Country: Great Britain
(Franklin Watts, 2013)

Sally Hewitt, *Project
Geography: Maps*
(Franklin Watts, 2013)

Websites

Mapskills (PowerPoint) –
Think Geography

www.thinkgeography.org.uk/Year%20
8%20Geog/.../Mapskills.ppt
This site explains map skills and
has lots of exercises to practise
your map skills.

Ordnance Survey Mapzone:

http://mapzone ordnancesurvey co.uk/
Log on to Ordnance Survey
Mapzone for online games,
free maps and information
about top tourist attractions
in Britain.

Maps for Kids – World map:

www.mapsofworld.com/kids
Maps for Kids website allows
you to explore the world
through maps, globes, puzzles,
games and more.

Index